César Chávez

Protecting Farm Workers

Stephanie E. Macceca

Consultant

Glenn Manns, M.A.
Teaching American History Coordinator
Ohio Valley Educational Cooperative

Publishing Credits

Dona Herweck Rice, *Editor-in-Chief*; Lee Aucoin, *Creative Director*; Conni Medina, M.A.Ed., *Editorial Director*; Jamey Acosta, *Associate Editor*; Neri Garcia, *Senior Designer*; Stephanie Reid, *Photo Researcher*; Rachelle Cracchiolo, M.A.Ed., *Publisher*

Image Credits

Teacher Created Materials

5301 Oceanus Drive
Huntington Beach, CA 92649-1030
http://www.tcmpub.com

ISBN 978-1-4333-1590-9
©2011 Teacher Created Materials, Inc.
Printed in China

Table of Contents

Childhood

César Chávez was born in Yuma, Arizona. He was born on March 31, 1927. There were six children in his family.

Yuma, Arizona

César as a young boy

As a child, César lived on a farm. He helped with the farm chores. He fed animals and gathered eggs. He learned that hard work was important.

A young boy picking tomatoes

The Chávez family farm was 100 acres. That is about the size of 100 football fields!

Chávez family farm

The Chávez family hired helpers to pick the crops on their farm. These helpers moved from farm to farm. They are called **migrant** (MY-gruhnt) **workers**.

Migrant workers picking crops

Picking crops is
hard on your back.

When César was 10, it did not rain for almost a year. The crops did not grow. The Chávez family had nothing to sell.

During a **drought**, the ground can get so dry that it cracks!

Without water, crops usually die.

There was no help for the Chávez family. Times were hard for everyone. Many people lost their jobs. People could not buy food. This time was known as the **Great Depression** (dih-PRESH-uhn).

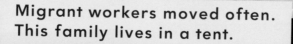

Migrant workers moved often. This family lives in a tent.

These men are standing in line to get a free bowl of soup.

Farm Work

The Chávez family became very poor. They lost their farm and their home. To make money, they became migrant workers. They moved from farm to farm to pick crops.

Fun Fact

César went to 37 schools! He had to quit school in the eighth grade.

A classroom in the 1930s during the Great Depression

Migrant workers on a farm

Picking crops was hard work. In the fields, there was no water to drink. There was no bathroom. The Chávez family worked hard. But they did not make much money.

This family works together in the fields.

Sometimes all eight members of the Chávez family lived in their car.

The Chávez family lived in a car like this one.

Making Things Better

As César grew up, he wanted to help migrant workers. He said that they should be paid more. He said that they needed clean water and bathrooms.

César gives a speech.

Many people listened to César.

César **protested** for workers' rights. He marched and gave speeches. He started a group to speak out about unfair rules for workers. Today, we call this group a **union**.

César speaking to news reporters

Once, César did not eat for 36 days. This made people listen to him.

César told people to boycott (BOI-kot) grapes. To boycott grapes means not to buy them.

In 1975, César made changes. The migrant workers had to use tools that hurt their backs. César got rid of those tools. He made sure migrant workers had water to drink and toilets to use in the fields.

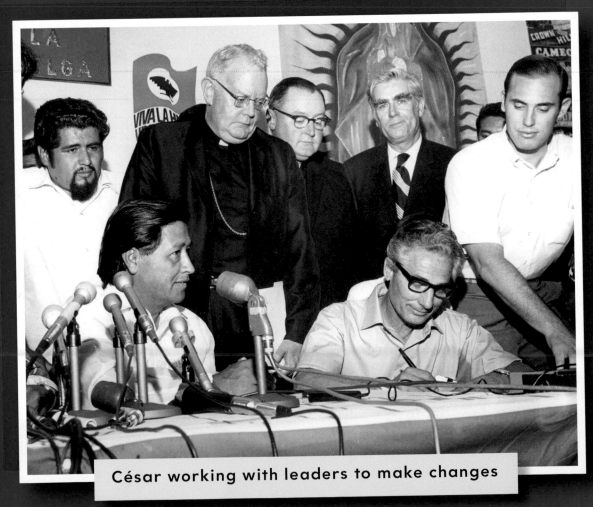

César working with leaders to make changes

Migrant workers had to use short-handled hoes.

A migrant farmer picks crops.

César made the farmers stop using bad poisons in the fields. These poisons are called **pesticides**. Pesticides kill bugs that eat crops. But they were not good for the workers.

A farm worker spraying pesticides

A gas mask

Pesticides can make a person sick. This farm worker wears a mask while he works.

César died on April 23, 1993. People in California celebrate his birthday. They remember how he helped migrant workers.

A statue of César

In Los Angeles, California, people named a street after César.

1927
César is born in Arizona.

1939
César becomes a migrant worker.

1962
César founds the United Farm Workers of America union.

Line

1975
César makes changes to help farmers.

1988
César goes on a hunger strike for 36 days against pesticides.

1993
César dies at the age of 66.

Glossary

boycott—to not buy from or give business to

drought—a long time without rain

Great Depression—a time during the 1930s when many people could not find a job and did not have a lot of money

migrant workers—people who move around from job to job

pesticides—chemicals that kill bugs that eat crops

protest—to speak out against something you think is not fair

union—a group of people that works to make things fair for its members

Index

Americans Today

This man is a migrant worker. He picks crops by hand. Thanks to César's work, his job is much easier!